POCKET SCIENCE

Lipid disorders

Jonathan Morrell MB BChir FRCGP DCH DRCOG

General Practitioner, Hastings

Hospital Practitioner, Conquest Hospital, Hastings, England

Author: Dr Jonathan Morrell
Copy Editor: Helen Barham
Layout: Joanne Laurie
Indexer: Laurence Errington
Operations: Julia Savory
Publishing Director: Julian Grover
Publisher: Stephen I'Anson

© CSF Medical Communications Ltd 2008
Eagle Tower
Montpellier Drive
Cheltenham
Gloucestershire
GL50 1TA
Tel: 01242 223890
Fax: 01242 243406
Email: *enquiries@csfmedical.com*
www.csfmedical.com

ISBN: 978-1-905466-79-5

Typeset by Creative, Paisley.
Printed and bound in Great Britain.

Contents

Preface

John Betteridge BSc PhD MD FRCP FAHA
Professor of Endocrinology and Metabolism
University College, London

Over the last decade or so there have been enormous developments in the field of cardiovascular protection through lipid lowering. The relationship of LDL-cholesterol to atherosclerotic disease can be considered to be causal because of the strength, consistency and independence of the epidemiological association, the understanding of the role of LDL in the atherosclerotic process and, importantly, a wealth of robust randomised controlled trials (RCTs) of well-tolerated and relatively safe drugs in a variety of at-risk populations showing highly significant benefit for cardiovascular disease (CVD) reduction.

Originally the province of a small number of specialist lipid clinics, management of lipid disorders, and particularly elevated LDL-cholesterol has moved mainly to primary care in a similar way to the management of hypertension a decade earlier. This is the result of the availability of the statin class of drugs which have proved to be amongst the most effective and well-tolerated drugs in any branch of medicine. The database from RCTs on which to base therapy is enormous, allowing cost benefit to be calculated and therapy to be targeted to increasing numbers of patient groups.

These developments provide a huge challenge to the primary care team but a potentially rewarding one given the proven ability to decrease the massive burden of ill health due to complications of

CVD. It is important to consider CVD as opposed to just coronary heart disease as lipid-lowering therapy has proved to reduce strokes as well as coronary events.

Dr Jonathan Morrell has been a pioneer in the organisation of effective CVD prevention in primary care and a highly effective communicator on the subject. In this new book he provides not only an up-to-date review of the background science but a practical hands-on approach to the effective implementation of evidence-based practice for the primary care team. This book should feature in every primary care centre as a source of information and as a stimulus to improved patient management.

In a way statins have been a victim of their own success and issues such as the cost of implementation of therapy have led to disagreements between budget holders and specialist opinion. Furthermore, barely a week goes by without some ill-informed attack in the lay press on the "dangers" of the statins. However, evidence of the clinical and cost benefit of interventions to control lipids continues to accumulate and informs official guidance on the use of the statins and other treatments options. Notably, as this book went to press towards the end of 2007 the National Institute for Health and Clinical Excellence (NICE) published its Final Appraisal Document that details the basis upon which it recommends the use of ezetimibe for the treatment of primary hypercholesterolaemia.

This timely book aims to enlighten primary care on this and other issues to enable what is above all the most important objective, to translate what has been learned in RCTs to the benefit of individual patients.

Introduction

What do we mean by lipid disorders?

Lipid disorders are metabolic disorders that lead to abnormal amounts of lipids in the body. An association between cholesterol and atherosclerosis has been recognised since the 1950s, and because cardiovascular disease (CVD) is a major cause of death worldwide, the field has been the focus of a lot of research. It is now clear that whilst a high total cholesterol level is associated with CVD, the type of lipoprotein that carries the cholesterol is also important, and not all lipoprotein fractions are harmful. In particular, although high levels of low-density lipoprotein cholesterol (LDL-C) are a risk factor for CVD, high levels of high-density lipoprotein cholesterol (HDL-C) confer a protective effect and low levels are a risk factor. There appears to be an independent association between high triglyceride levels and CVD.

These points need to be borne in mind when considering terminology to describe lipid disorders. Hyperlipidaemia refers to raised blood levels of one or more of total cholesterol, LDL-C and triglycerides. Dyslipidaemia is a broader term and encompasses hyperlipidaemia and/or low levels of HDL-C. Mixed dyslipidaemia denotes concurrent hyperlipidaemia and low HDL-C. Mixed hyperlipidaemia denotes raised total cholesterol and triglycerides. Hypercholesterolaemia refers to a high total cholesterol level.

It is also worth noting that the relationship between lipid levels and CVD risk is continuous and almost linear, and although particular lipid levels are recommended as desirable targets, there is no absolute cut-off that defines a normal or abnormal lipid level.

Why are lipid disorders important?

High levels of cholesterol, in particular high levels of LDL-C, appear to play a pivotal role in the development of coronary heart disease (CHD). Low levels of HDL-C and raised levels of triglycerides are also independent risk factors for CHD (Figure 1). CHD is a major cause of illness and death in the UK; modifying lipid levels can reduce morbidity and mortality.

Reduction of plasma LDL-C is key to reducing cardiovascular morbidity and mortality, and this can be achieved through both lifestyle modification and pharmacological interventions. However, other cardiovascular risk factors must be taken into account when assessing a patient's overall risk for CHD.

An emerging role for primary care

Treatment of lipid disorders has become a mainstream activity for all primary care professionals. This has come about because of:

- increased understanding of the role of lipid disorders in causing both CHD and more widespread CVD;
- the growing burden of CVD to society in general;

Figure 1.
High levels of low-density lipoprotein cholesterol (LDL-C) and triglycerides, and low levels of high-density lipoprotein cholesterol (HDL-C) appear to play a pivotal role in the development of coronary heart disease (CHD).

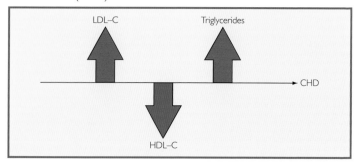

- incontrovertible evidence from clinical trials of the benefits of modifying patients' lipid profiles in terms of reducing both morbidity and mortality;
- the ability to manage lipid disorders effectively in everyday practice;
- the influence of national directives and performance reward schemes that recognise the importance of lipid modification in the prevention of CVD.

Primary care teams are thus responsible for:

- assignment of appropriate cholesterol tests;
- diagnosis of lipid disorders;
- assessment of cardiovascular risk;
- deciding on the most appropriate interventions for individual patients;
- selecting a lipid-lowering drug regimen if indicated;
- treating to target lipid levels;
- organisation of regular follow-up to manage complications and maximise adherence to treatment.

Primary care professionals therefore need to develop practical strategies to manage and maintain appropriate levels of care for their patients with lipid disorders.

About this book

Pocket Science – Lipid disorders provides health professionals with a review of the evidence available on lipid disorders, together with practical clinical information relevant to the management of patients in the primary care setting. Because of the way that the evidence base has accumulated over the years, much of the data available refers specifically to CHD. The term CVD is often used in clinical papers as an encompassing term; where it is not clear what is included or excluded, we have assumed that CVD refers to CHD, stroke and 'other cardiovascular diseases'.

Lipid disorders: facts and figures

Key points

- Coronary heart disease (CHD) is the most common cause of death in the UK.

- The UK has one of the highest death rates from CHD amongst developed Western countries.

- CHD cost the UK economy almost £8 billion in 2003 and CVD almost £26 billion.[1]

- Of the overall cost of CHD to the NHS in 2003, 16.4% was for medications and 78.6% for inpatient care. [1]

- Effective interventions are available to reduce CHD and its burden on the NHS and the economy as a whole.

- Cholesterol, in particular raised plasma levels of low-density lipoprotein cholesterol (LDL-C), is a pivotal risk factor for CHD.

- Reducing LDL-C reduces cardiovascular disease (CVD).

Epidemiology

Coronary heart disease is the most common cause of death in the UK

In the UK in 2005:

- CVD caused just over 208,000 deaths;[2] this is like wiping out the population of Norwich or Swansea every year;
- CHD was responsible for approximately one-half of all deaths from CVD, and stroke for one-quarter;
- CHD alone was the most common cause of death, accounting for about one-fifth of male deaths and one-sixth of female deaths (almost 101,000 deaths in total).

It is predicted that, globally, deaths from cardiovascular disease will increase from 16.7 million in 2002 to 23.3 million in 2030,[3] which is roughly equivalent to the population of Australia.

The UK has one of the highest death rates for CHD among developed Western countries

Mortality from CHD has decreased gradually but steadily since the early 1970s, as risk factors have been addressed and medical therapy has improved. In the last 10 years the prevalence of CHD in adults under 65 years of age in England has fallen by 46% (Figure 2), and similar reductions in deaths from CHD and stroke have occurred for those aged 65 years or older.[2]

In recent years death rates have been falling fastest in those aged 55 years and above, but more slowly in younger people. For example, in the decade 1995 to 2005, deaths from CHD in men aged 55–64 years in the UK fell by 50%, compared with 27% in men aged 35–44 years. In women aged 55–64 years there was a 56% fall and in those aged 35–44 years a 20% fall.

Figure 2.
Death rates for coronary heart disease in people under 65 years of age in England from 1970 to 2004.[2]

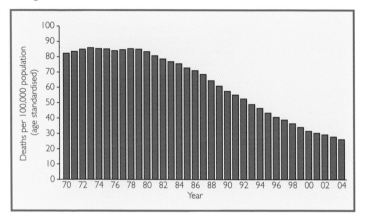

Death rates from stroke fell throughout the latter part of the last century, and for people under 65 years decreased by 23% between 1995 and 2005. Recently, however, rates have declined more slowly than previously, particularly in the younger age groups.[2]

The UK lags behind many other countries in the prevention and treatment of CHD. Amongst Western European countries, only Ireland and Finland have higher death rates for CHD than the UK (Figure 3).[2] Given the numbers of people affected and the availability of interventions that have been proven effective, there is still enormous scope to do more to prevent deaths from CVD.

Public health targets have been set for the reduction of CVD for England, Scotland, Wales and Northern Ireland.[4–7]

- In England, the aim is to reduce the death rate from CVD by 40% by 2010.[4]
- In Scotland the aim is to reduce mortality from CHD in those under 75 years of age by 60% between 1995 and 2010.[5]

Figure 3.
Country-specific mortality rates for coronary heart disease in men and women aged 35–74 years in 2000.[10]

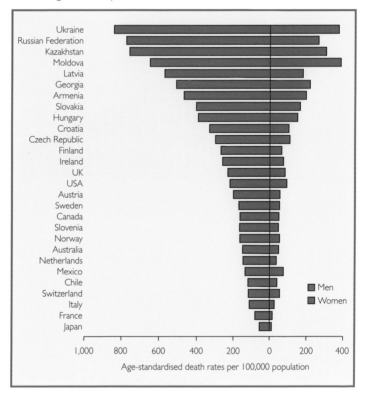

Economic burden of CHD

CHD has a huge economic burden

The costs of CHD and CVD to the NHS in 2003 were over £3.5 billion and £14.7 billion, respectively, over 75% of which was for inpatient care. Less than 18% of these costs were for medications.[3] The overall cost to the economy in the same period, including the cost to the NHS and estimates for loss of productivity and for informal care, was estimated at £26 billion for CVD and £7.9 billion for CHD.[3]

The link between blood lipids and CHD

Risk factors for CHD are multiple and include:

- age;
- sex;
- genetic predisposition (including family history and ethnic origin);
- lipid disorders;
- hypertension;
- smoking;
- diabetes, obesity and the metabolic syndrome;
- psychosocial factors;
- diet;
- lack of physical activity.

> **Cholesterol, in particular raised LDL-C, is a pivotal risk factor for CHD**

Although most coronary events can be explained on the basis of blood lipid levels, blood pressure, smoking and diabetes, the available data identify high LDL-C as the pivotal risk factor for CHD.[8] In populations with relatively low levels of LDL-C, such as in China and Japan, the incidence of CHD remains low, even when smoking and hypertension are highly prevalent.[8]

The National Heart Forum has suggested that high blood cholesterol (>5.2 mmol/L) is responsible for the greatest proportion (46%) of cases of CHD in the UK – compared with 37% for physical inactivity, 19% for smoking, 13% for high blood pressure (>140/90 mmHg) and 6% for obesity.[9] These findings are supported by data from the USA, which showed that high blood cholesterol (>5.2 mmol/L) was responsible for the greatest proportion (43%) of cases of CHD.[10] In 2002, the World Health Report estimated that, in developed countries, 60% of CHD and nearly 40% of ischaemic strokes are due to cholesterol levels in excess of a theoretical maximum of 3.8 mmol/L.[11]

Most of the common risk factors for CHD can be eliminated or modified: high LDL-C levels and blood pressure can be reduced, smoking can be stopped, physical activity can be increased and healthier diets adopted. So, whilst CVD is a huge problem, for many patients it can be prevented, or at least delayed.

Reducing cholesterol reduces CHD

There is now little doubt that lowering blood cholesterol reduces cardiovascular mortality and morbidity. In the 1994 landmark Scandinavian Simvastatin Survival Study (4S), reduction in total cholesterol of 25% and in LDL-C of 35%, and an 8% increase in HDL-C, in patients treated with simvastatin correlated with improved survival rates compared with the placebo group.[12] Analysis of these results indicates that treatment of 100 CHD patients with simvastatin for 6 years would achieve the following benefits:

- prevention of 4 out of 9 deaths from CHD;
- prevention of non-fatal myocardial infarction in 7 out of 21 patients;
- avoidance of revascularisation in 6 out of 19 patients.[13]

Since 4S, many other trials and meta-analyses have added credence to these findings, such that we can now be confident that reducing serum levels of LDL-C by a variety of pharmacological and non-pharmacological interventions reduces the incidence of CVD.

We can now be confident that reducing serum levels of LDL-C...reduces the incidence of CVD

The Cholesterol Treatment Trialists' Collaboration estimated from clinical trials that every 1 mmol/L lowering of LDL-C resulted in 12% fewer deaths, 19% fewer CHD events and 17% fewer strokes.[14]

Pathophysiology

Cholesterol accumulation leads to atherosclerosis

Simplistically, atherosclerosis refers to a narrowing or hardening of the arteries as cholesterol accumulates within the vascular wall. In reality, it is a complex multifactorial disease. Atherosclerotic lesions reduce blood flow and consequently oxygen supply to target organs; in the heart this results in damage to the myocardium. This process is commonly referred to as CHD, although this term is somewhat tautological; coronary artery disease (CAD) would appear to be a better description.

Lipid is transported in the plasma within lipoprotein particles of differing densities and composition. Exogenous pathways of lipoprotein metabolism deal with the packaging of fat derived from the diet, whereas endogenous pathways are involved in the production of lipoproteins (very-low-density lipoprotein [VLDL] and LDL) in the liver and bloodstream. These pathways are summarised in Figures 4 and 5.

Figure 4.

The exogenous pathway of lipid metabolism.

(A) Dietary fats and lipids are broken down in the gastrointestinal tract into cholesterol, fatty acids and mono- and diglycerides. These are combined with bile acids to form water-soluble micelles that carry lipids to absorptive sites in the duodenum.

(B) Chylomicrons are formed at the duodenal absorptive sites, and enter the bloodstream for transportation to the liver.

(C) Chylomicrons are hydrolysed rapidly by the enzyme lipoprotein lipase (LPL), releasing the triglyceride (TG) core, free fatty acids and mono- and diglycerides for energy production or storage.

(D) The cholesterol-rich residue (chylomicron remnant) undergoes further delipidation. These are taken up by the liver, undergo lysosomal degradation, and are either used for cell membrane synthesis or excreted as bile salts.

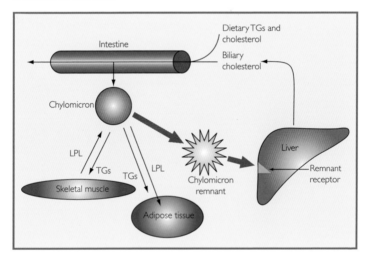

Figure 5.

The endogenous pathway of lipid metabolism.

(A) Very low density lipoprotein (VLDL) transports endogenous lipids from the liver to most tissues for oxidation or storage.

(B) Triglycerides are transported from the liver to adipose tissues by VLDL. VLDL particles are transformed to form cholesterol-rich low density lipoprotein (LDL) by lipoprotein lipase (LPL) and/or hepatic lipase via intermediate density lipoprotein (IDL).

(C) LDL exists as a number of subfractions (LDL I–IV) of varying atherogenicity.

(D) LDL can be absorbed by macrophages within the arterial cell wall to form lipid-rich foam cells, the initial stage in the pathogenesis of atherosclerotic plaques.

(E) High density lipoprotein (HDL) removes excess free cholesterol (Chol) in peripheral tissues (e.g. macrophages in the arterial wall) and returns it to the liver where it is excreted in bile.

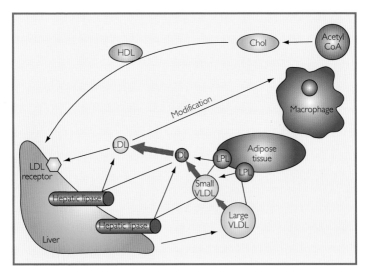

Why is LDL 'bad cholesterol'?

Oxidised LDL is involved in the formation of fatty streaks

Atherosclerosis is now known to be an oxidative and inflammatory disease, and oxidation of LDL plays a pivotal role in its onset. Oxidised LDL is not recognised by native LDL receptors in the vasculature and instead is taken up by scavenger receptors, which have no intrinsic feedback control mechanism. Thus, oxidised LDL is taken up uncontrollably, principally by macrophages to form foam cells, which eventually die off, releasing cholesterol which accumulates within the subendothelial space to form fatty streaks. The fatty streak enlarges as more cholesterol is deposited, along with cellular debris and collagen from smooth muscle cells, until a frank atherosclerotic plaque is formed. In addition, oxidised LDL promotes the release of inflammatory mediators, which are also implicated in the pathogenesis of CHD.

HDL prevents the formation of fatty streaks

Why is HDL 'good cholesterol'?

HDL removes cholesterol from peripheral tissues and cells (including macrophages) and transports it to the liver, thereby combating the formation of foam cells. In addition, paraoxonase, an intrinsic antioxidant enzyme of HDL, has been shown to protect HDL from oxidation, thereby preserving its function. It also inhibits the formation of oxidised LDL. Thus, high levels of HDL may be beneficial by increasing cholesterol transport to the liver and reducing the consequences of oxidation.[15,16]

Although epidemiological data and evidence from animal studies for the importance of HDL-C are strong, evidence from clinical trials that raising HDL-C is beneficial is lacking. Infusion of hyperfunctional apolipoprotein A-1 Milano had positive effects, but other trials, including early experience with inhibitors of cholesterol ester transfer protein, have not proved the concept.[17]

How are triglycerides involved?

High blood levels of triglycerides have also been implicated in an increased incidence of CHD, though this association appears to be less strong than the link between LDL-C and CHD, and becomes much weaker when other risk factors are taken into account.[18] The link between triglyceride levels and increased CHD risk is complex and may be related to low levels of HDL-C, highly atherogenic forms of LDL-C, or both.[18]

NOTES

Clinical presentation and diagnosis

Key points

- A broad spectrum of lipid disorders are characterised by levels of plasma lipoproteins.

- The full lipoprotein profile should be checked, not just total cholesterol.

- Assessment of lipid profile should constitute just a part of a total cardiovascular risk assessment for any individual patient.

- Risk factors for CHD interact to exert a much greater combined coronary risk and tend to cluster in individuals.

Types of lipid disorder

A full lipid profile should guide treatment selection

Raised plasma LDL-C is just one type of lipid disorder. A broad spectrum of syndromes are characterised by abnormal or deranged plasma lipid profiles, all of which increase the risk for the development of CHD. Table 1 shows the World Health Organization (WHO)/Fredrickson classification of the most common lipid abnormalities.[19] In terms of clinical management, these disorders are all characterised by raised total plasma cholesterol and/or raised plasma triglycerides, and on this basis may be treated with appropriate lipid-lowering therapy.

Table 1.
World Health Organization (WHO)/Fredrickson classification of dyslipidaemias.[3]

Type	Overnight serum	Elevated lipoproteins
I	Creamy top layer	CM
IIa	Clear	LDL
IIb	Clear	LDL, VLDL
III	Turbid	IDL
IV	Turbid	VLDL
V	Creamy top layer, turbid bottom	CM, VLDL

CM, chylomicron; IDL, intermediate density lipoproteins; LDL, low density lipoprotein; VLDL, very low density lipoprotein.

It is important to check a patient's individual lipoprotein fractions (LDL-C, HDL-C and triglycerides) rather than just measuring total cholesterol, in order to diagnose the relevant dyslipidaemia and therefore decide on the appropriate clinical treatment.[20]

What are 'normal' levels of cholesterol?

Cholesterol and triglyceride levels show a wide range across the population, and levels vary between countries. Although 'normal' levels can be defined in relation to the overall levels in the population, this is not particularly helpful, especially when the lipid profiles of a population as a whole are elevated, as is the case in the UK.

Associated clinical disorders	Serum total cholesterol	Serum total triglyceride
LPL deficiency Apo-CII deficiency	N	++
Familial and polygenic hypercholesterolaemia, nephrosis, hypothyroidism, familial combined hyperlipidaemia	++	N
Familial combined hyperlipidaemia	++	+
Dysbetalipoproteinaemia	+	+
Familial hypertriglyceridaemia Familial combined hyperlipidaemia Sporadic hypertriglyceridaemia Diabetes	N+	++
Diabetes Familial LPL deficiency	+	++

Apo-CII, apolipoprotein CII; LPL, lipoprotein lipase; +, increased; ++, greatly increased; N, normal; N+, normal or increased.

In the UK about 70% of adults have cholesterol levels above 5.0 mmol/L.[21] Values of cholesterol are 1.0–1.5 mmol/L lower in childhood and rise to adult levels after puberty. Cholesterol levels are similar in men and women, although women generally have higher HDL-C levels contributing to their total cholesterol. In women, cholesterol levels tend to rise after the menopause to a mean level that is a little higher than in men. Levels of cholesterol and LDL-C are maintained at substantially higher levels than is essential for health, even in communities that have relatively low mean values, such as in Japan and China.

> **Perhaps 'normal' cholesterol levels should be defined as those at which maintenance of health is optimal and illness is minimised**

Perhaps 'normal' cholesterol levels should be defined as those at which maintenance of health is optimal and illness is minimised. In epidemiological studies within and across communities there is a continuous relationship between cholesterol levels and both cardiovascular and total mortality. The relationship follows a continuous, semi-log-linear pattern, and there is no evidence of a threshold cholesterol level below which there is no evidence of harm.

Patient assessment

> **Assessment of total cardiovascular risk is essential**

Although lipid levels are a key risk factor for CVD, cardiovascular risk factors interact with one another to exert a much greater combined risk. In addition, risk factors tend to cluster in individuals. It is therefore vital that a proper cardiovascular risk assessment is performed for each patient before making a decision to intervene.[8]

In terms of secondary prevention, the decision to treat is straightforward. Diabetes should be treated as a CHD risk-equivalent. CHD risk-equivalents carry a risk for major coronary events equal to the risk associated with the presence of established CHD (i.e. high risk). In some cases, life-expectancy and comorbidities also have to be considered, particularly when assessing the elderly.

In terms of primary prevention, the 10-year cardiovascular event risk can be calculated using Framingham-based risk function charts, such as those produced by the Joint British Societies (JBS) and the British Hypertension Society (BHS). The British Heart Foundation has developed a computerised version of the mathematical function to allow more accurate calculation (available on CD-ROM). The risk prediction charts are based on sex, age, smoking status, systolic blood pressure and the ratio of total cholesterol to HDL-C. Male sex, increasing age, history of smoking, elevated systolic blood pressure and higher total cholesterol : HDL-C ratios are associated with increased risk.

Framingham-based scores may overestimate current cardiovascular risk in European populations, because they reflect the higher risk of cardiovascular disease in the US in the 1970s and 1980s. They also do not take into account family history or socioeconomic status. A new cardiovascular risk score, QRISK, may provide more accurate risk estimations for the UK population based on age, sex and level of social deprivation; however, additional validation is required.[22] At present, however, Framingham-based scores remain the standard.

Intervention is recommended at a 10-year risk of CVD of 20%

The threshold at which intervention is recommended is a 10-year risk of CVD of 20%, which is approximately equivalent to a 10-year CHD risk of 15%. Patients whose 10-year CVD risk is 10–20% (10-year CHD risk 10–15%) are at moderately increased risk, and some of these patients may benefit from treatment, although they are not considered a priority compared with high-risk patients.

Given clear evidence of a benefit of treatment with statins, in 2004 the UK Government sanctioned the sale of low-dose simvastatin (10 mg) direct to consumers under pharmacist control. It is licensed for use in patients at moderate risk of CHD (10–15% 10-year risk) and may lower LDL-C by around 27%, although clinical trials have not been conducted with this dose in patients at moderate risk. Pharmacists do not have to measure cholesterol levels before treatment, although it is considered good practice to do so. Pharmacists are advised to recommend that patients taking the drug inform their GP, and provide them with any test results they have.[23] Uptake has been low to date, possibly in part because people prefer to see their GP first.[24]

When assessing abnormal lipid levels it is important to consider secondary causes of dyslipidaemia, which commonly include obesity, diabetes and excessive alcohol intake. Measurement of fasting blood glucose, thyroid stimulating hormone concentration (to rule out hypothyroidism) and liver function tests are useful investigations before initiating treatment.

NOTES

NOTES

Patient management

Key points

- Patients should be treated according to the extent of their cardiovascular risk, not just according to their lipid profile.

- Lifestyle modifications (e.g. smoking cessation, improved diet and increased exercise) can have beneficial effects on a range of cardiovascular risk factors.

- The primary goal is the reduction of LDL-C.

- If lifestyle changes alone do not lower LDL-C levels satisfactorily, pharmacological intervention may be justified.

- Statins are the first-line agents for treating most lipid disorders. They produce small increases in HDL-C and also have a moderate effect in reducing plasma triglycerides.

- NICE guidance is now available on ezetimibe, the cholesterol absorption inhibitor. Ezetimibe provides additive LDL-C-lowering efficacy when combined with statins. It also has small effects on triglyceride and HDL-C levels.

- Fibrates are particularly effective in reducing triglyceride levels and also have beneficial effects on HDL-C and LDL-C.

Lessons from the evidence base

1. Treating to global cardiovascular risk is important

Primary prevention can be as important as secondary prevention for some patients

A series of landmark trials during the last decade has established the evidence base for lipid lowering in patients across a broad spectrum of cardiovascular risk. Although early trials followed the clinical dichotomy of primary and secondary prevention, the concept of a global cardiovascular risk continuum has now begun to emerge.

An individual's cardiovascular risk is determined not by isolated levels of single risk factors but by the composite interaction of them all. This was classically illustrated by Haffner's work in Finland, where he showed that the 7-year CHD event rate in patients with type 2 diabetes without prior MI was the equivalent of that in non-diabetic subjects who had already suffered an event. In other words, the risk in a primary-prevention population can be as high as in patients requiring secondary prevention.[25]

The Heart Protection Study (HPS) confirmed that lipid-lowering therapy should be targeted to a patient's global cardiovascular risk. In this study of high-risk individuals, patients with baseline cholesterol levels below 5.0 mmol/L (LDL-C levels < 3.0 or even 2.6 mmol/L) benefited from lipid lowering to the same degree as patients with higher entry values.[26] In addition, the benefits estimated in the Cholesterol Treatment Trialists' Collaboration were seen irrespective of age or starting cholesterol, LDL-C or HDL-C levels, thereby supporting the approach to treatment according to CV risk rather than absolute cholesterol values.[14]

2. The range of patients who can benefit from lipid lowering has been extended

The HPS also confirmed the value of lipid lowering in various groups hitherto not covered by the evidence base. Benefits were shown for women, patients over 75 years of age, those with atherosclerotic disease elsewhere (e.g. peripheral arterial disease and non-haemorrhagic stroke) and those with diabetes and metabolic syndrome. The findings thus extend the range of patients who are likely to benefit from treatment.

3. Lifestyle interventions are beneficial

The benefits of optimising weight, stopping smoking, increasing physical activity and eating a healthy diet are manifest. It should be remembered that clinical trials of lipid-lowering drugs are done with patients in whom lifestyle interventions have already been addressed.

Dietary modification has been shown to improve plasma lipid profiles. For example, an analysis of community-based trials in over 9,000 patients showed that the stage-I and -II diets developed by the US National Education Cholesterol Program (NCEP) significantly ($p<0.001$) decreased serum total cholesterol, LDL-C and triglycerides.[27] Diet alone often reduces LDL-C by more than 10% (in addition to the reduction achieved by drugs) and probably confers benefit through other mechanisms beyond lipid modification. Using a 'portfolio' of dietary measures (plant sterols, soy protein and viscous fibre) has been reported to decrease LDL-C by 29%.[28]

Another beneficial effect of low-fat diets is that they often result in weight loss, thus reducing obesity, another risk factor for CHD.[27]

A 5-year randomised trial showed that the combination of a low-cholesterol diet and smoking cessation advice in 1,232 patients (most of whom were smokers) reduced MI (combined fatal and non-fatal) and sudden death by 47% compared with the control group ($p=0.028$).[29]

4. The primary goal of lipid-lowering therapy is the reduction of LDL-C

Analysis of CHD secondary prevention activity at one Greek hospital showed that, compared with usual care, reducing LDL-C by 46% – that is, treating to the NCEP LDL-C target level of less than 2.6 mmol/L – halved the subsequent cardiovascular event rate in just 3 years.[30] Trials that demonstrate the largest differences with respect to reductions in LDL-C show the most positive outcomes. For example, in the HPS there was an average 0.96 mmol/L difference in LDL-C between the study groups over 5 years, and a significant reduction in major vascular events was achieved.[26] In contrast, in the lipid-lowering arm of the Antihypertensive and Lipid-Lowering Treatment to Prevent Heart Attack Trial (ALLHAT), which failed to achieve a significant difference in major events, the average between-group difference in LDL-C during the study was 0.57 mmol/L.[31]

With the availability of cholesterol-lowering medication that can achieve reductions in LDL-C of more than 1 mmol/L, clinical trials have been able to explore whether 'lower is better'. Four well-conducted clinical trials explored the value of driving LDL-C down to very low levels in high-risk people with CHD. A meta-analysis of these results confirms a significant 16% reduction in CHD death or non-fatal myocardial infarction in more aggressively treated patients;[32] it is this that has prompted the new lower target recommendations. At the moment, there appears to be no lower threshold at which LDL-C reduction ceases to confer benefit for individuals at cardiovascular risk. Speculation suggests that neonatal levels (around 1.0 mmol/L) might be the lowest point, and trials to test this have already been designed.

> **There appears to be no lower threshold at which LDL-C reduction ceases to confer benefit**

5. Statins are currently the most widely used drugs to manage lipid disorders

Treating to global cardiovascular risk means employing a range of interventions that are appropriate for individual patients. This means optimising blood pressure and blood sugar control, as well as the lipid profile, and using antiplatelet drugs as appropriate. Prescribing analyses show that most practitioners use statins.

Statins are the mainstay of treatment and are remarkably well tolerated. As patents expire, generic products are becoming available, with significant price reductions. Simvastatin, by virtue of its moderate potency, good tolerability and extensive evidence base is a natural first choice, although target values may not be achieved.

Different statin strategies can be used to achieve target values including increasing the dose at 4–6 week intervals, switching to more potent statins or using high doses of powerful statins to 'get it right first time'. Achieving more aggressive lipid targets implies the use of higher dose and more efficacious statin therapy. However, in their guidance issued towards the end of 2007, NICE recommends coadministering ezetimibe instead of switching from initial statin therapy where uptitration is limited by intolerance or fails to achieve target levels.[33] The NICE Committee agreed that this treatment option is a cost-effective use of NHS resources when compared with switching to an alternative statin.[33]

The growing evidence base for the statins has allowed a more rigorous assessment of their cost-effectiveness (Table 2). Even before the patents of simvastatin and prevastatin expire, the cost-effectiveness of statins is clearly well within the 'benchmark' for cost per life-years gained defined by NICE, and this explains the commitment of central government to fund the use of these drugs. Clinical trials show that, to be effective, statins need to be continued for several years before effects on outcomes become clear. Thus, primary care will need to meet the challenge of ensuring appropriate follow-up and compliance.

Table 2.
Implications of targeting statin treatment at four coronary heart disease (CHD) risk levels, showing the number needed to treat (NNT), cost-effectiveness and implications for the UK population.[34]

| | 1-year CHD risk level | | | |
	4.5%	**3.0%**	**2.0%**	**1.5%**
NNT (over 5 years)	13	20	30	40
Cost per life-year gained (£)	5,100	8,200	10,700	12,500
UK adults above threshold (%)	5.1	8.2	15.8	24.7
Annual cost (£ million)	549	885	1,712	2,673

6. An atherogenic lipoprotein profile can occur without raised LDL-C

Many patients with CVD do not have an obviously elevated LDL-C. However, a so-called atherogenic lipoprotein phenotype has been defined. This term describes dyslipidaemia that is characterised by low levels of HDL-C, raised triglycerides and a change in the structure of LDL-C towards a smaller, denser and more atherogenic version of the normal particle. This change in the quality of LDL-C occurs when triglyceride levels exceed 1.5–1.7 mmol/L and is mirrored by a similar change in the quality of HDL-C, which also becomes smaller and denser and possibly less cardioprotective.

The atherogenic lipoprotein profile is often seen in individuals with diabetes, insulin resistance or the metabolic syndrome. With the increasing prevalence of obesity and physical inactivity in society, prevalence of the metabolic syndrome has already reached 20–25%. The future cardiovascular consequences of this are clearly of enormous concern.

Whilst statins will reduce raised triglycerides, they are not very effective in raising HDL-C levels. Evidence from clinical trials that increasing HDL-C improves outcomes may not be that strong, but the compelling direct epidemiological relationship between HDL-C and

CHD has persuaded many experts to suggest an HDL-C target of greater than 1.0 mmol/L (>1.2 mmol/L in women) in situations where HDL-C is low. This also applies to patients who are already receiving statin therapy, and points to additional roles for fibrates and nicotinic acid to achieve this target. There is an urgent need for the use of these drugs to be defined by appropriate outcome studies, particularly in combination with statins.

7. Non-HDL-C reflects total atherogenic burden of the lipoprotein profile

Non-HDL-C is calculated by subtracting the HDL-C concentration from the total cholesterol concentration. This value identifies both the LDL-C and the triglyceride-rich lipoproteins, which are also atherogenic. Thus, non-HDL-C gives a more accurate reflection of the total atherogenic burden of the lipoprotein profile. It has already been adopted in US guidelines as a secondary target of therapy in individuals with high levels of triglycerides. It is a particularly useful parameter in patients with established vascular disease and mixed hyperlipidaemia.

Guidelines

The National Service Framework (NSF) on CHD sets out national standards for the prevention, diagnosis and management of CHD. The aim is to reduce death from CHD in people aged <75 years by 40% by 2010.[35]

Another aim is to reduce variations in healthcare across the country, as set out in the *Saving Lives* and *Choosing Health* white papers.[4, 36]

In 2005, the Joint British Societies (JBS) produced guidelines on the prevention of cardiovascular disease in clinical practice (JBS 2) which included target cholesterol levels and recommendations on lipid-lowering therapy (Box 1).[37]

Box 1.

Risk factor management for patients with, or at risk of, CVD. Targets recommended by JBS 2.[37]

- Smoking cessation.
- Waist circumference <102 cm in men (<92 cm for Asian men) and <88 cm in women (<78 cm for Asian women).
- Body mass index <25 kg/m^2.
- Blood pressure <140/85 mmHg (<130/80 mmHg in those with established CVD, diabetes or chronic renal failure).
- Total cholesterol <4 mmol/L (or 25% reduction, whichever is lower).
- LDL-C <2 mmol/L (or 30% reduction, whichever is lower).
- Fasting glucose <6.1 mmol/L.
- HbA$_{1C}$ <6.5% (diabetics).
- Use of cardioprotective drugs where appropriate (e.g. antihypertensive, antithrombotic, lipid-lowering or glucose-lowering therapies).

NICE has produced guidance specifically on starting statin therapy in adults with CVD, or at risk of CVD,[38] and has also issued guidance covering the management of blood lipids in patients with type 2 diabetes.[39] Further guidance from NICE on cardiovascular risk assessment and lipid modification is due to be published at the beginning of 2008; a draft version for consultation was published in June 2007.[40]

The US NCEP guideline on high blood cholesterol also provides useful information on the diagnosis and treatment of lipid disorders.[20]

Lipid targets

Intervention points and targets are recommended in guidelines

National Service Framework

The UK NSF for CHD specifies that high-risk patients should receive dietary advice and pharmacotherapy to lower total cholesterol to below 5.0 mmol/L (or by 20–25%, whichever is lower) and to lower serum LDL-C to below 3.0 mmol/L (or by 30%, whichever is lower).[35]

NCEP

The NCEP recommends LDL-C level as the primary target for diagnosis and intervention. Therapy should start when LDL-C is above 1.8–4.1 mmol/L, depending on an individual's cardiovascular risk status.[20,41]

JBS 2

The recently published JBS 2 guidelines establish more stringent targets for plasma cholesterol levels than those published previously. These targets are equally applicable to patients with established CVD, those at risk of CVD (cardiovascular risk ≥20% over 10 years) and those with diabetes.

The targets are total cholesterol below 4 mmol/L, plus LDL-C below 2 mmol/L, or a 25% reduction from baseline in total cholesterol plus a 30% reduction from baseline in LDL-C (whichever achieves a lower absolute value).

It should be noted that the official national targets for cholesterol levels have not altered since the publication of JBS2, and currently remain as stated in the NSF. The total cholesterol target in the Quality and Outcomes Framework (QOF) remains 5 mmol/L.

Firm targets for HDL-C and triglyceride values were not set, but 'desirable values' given were:

- non-HDL-C below 3.0 mmol/L;
- HDL-C above 1.0 mmol/L for men; 1.2 mmol/L for women;
- triglycerides below 1.7 mmol/L.[37]

The decision to start lipid-lowering therapy should be made as part of the assessment of total cardiovascular risk. People with established atherosclerotic disease, or who are at high risk of CVD (cardiovascular risk ≥20% over 10 years) or who have diabetes mellitus should be offered lipid-lowering therapy, irrespective of their baseline lipid levels. People with particularly elevated individual risk factors are also at high risk of CVD. For example, those with a total cholesterol:HDL-C ratio of 6 or higher, or familial dyslipidaemia, should be offered lipid-lowering therapy.[37]

NICE

The NICE guidance on statins recommends commencing statin therapy in patients with clinical CVD and also in those who have a risk of developing CVD in the next 10 years of 20% or higher, which is consistent with the JBS 2 guidelines.[38] The NICE guidance on ezetimibe should be read in conjunction with the advice on statins.[33]

Lipid targets need to be interpreted appropriately

The NSF targets, although relatively straightforward, are frequently poorly interpreted, to the disadvantage of some patients. The majority of practitioners aim to achieve the headline target for total cholesterol, and pay little attention to LDL-C, the concept of percentage reduction or the subtleties of the lipoprotein profile. Unfortunately, however, it is possible to achieve the target total cholesterol concentration but without achieving the target for LDL-C, particularly in patients with low HDL-C. Consider, for example, a patient with a total cholesterol level of 4.8 mmol/L but a low HDL-C level of 0.7 mmol/L and triglycerides of 2.0 mmol/L. The calculated LDL-C level determined using the Friedewald formula is 3.2 mmol/L, which is still too high. It is for this reason that the US NCEP guidelines use LDL-C alone and do not refer to total cholesterol levels.

The concept of percentage reduction was introduced to ensure satisfactory reductions of total cholesterol and LDL-C in treated patients. Lessons from trials (and the Cholesterol Treatment Trialists' Collaboration) show us that reducing total cholesterol from 5.1 mmol/L to 4.9 mmol/L, for example, is unlikely to produce significant benefit.[14] For such a patient, aiming for a percentage reduction would be more beneficial, and is more in keeping with the evidence base. However, use of percentage reduction is difficult to audit, and in reality is rarely undertaken in primary care, where treatment to targets is favoured.

With the current focus on achieving lipid targets, it should be borne in mind that the targets are derived by consensus panels and have little supportive evidence from clinical outcome trials per se. Many patients in the clinical trials did not achieve target levels, yet, presumably, derived benefit from treatment. However, new evidence from Scotland shows that treating to target in a 'therapeutic alliance' fostered between patient and health professionals in primary care is 2.5 times more likely to achieve target values than a 'fire and forget' approach.[42]

As prescribers we must therefore use our clinical judgement and weigh up the benefit from the specific settings of randomised trials with the extrapolated benefit derived from the relative surrogate of achieving target lipid values. In addition, the healthcare benefits arising from the achievement of lower targets need to be considered in the context of balancing manifold priorities, all with cost and resource requirements.

Management strategies

Lifestyle changes

Substantial evidence supports the beneficial effects of a wide array of lifestyle changes on an individual's cardiovascular risk status (Box 2).

Lifestyle changes can affect a range of cardiovascular risk factors

Although a reduction in LDL-C is the primary target for treatment of dyslipidaemia, it should be remembered that cardiovascular disorders are caused by a variety of factors. Thus, tackling any one risk factor in isolation, even one as critical as LDL-C, is unlikely to be sufficient.[8] Any intervention strategy should include lifestyle changes. Indeed, a multifactorial approach that involves incorporating a healthy diet, exercise and smoking cessation is the first-line intervention recommended by most clinicians, and appears to be justified from the available evidence.[8] Unfortunately, however, lifestyle measures are often poorly implemented in practice, through lack of expertise, time and conviction.

Box 2.
Lifestyle changes that reduce cardiovascular risk factors

- Smoking cessation.
- Increased physical activity.
- Dietary changes to reduce weight if necessary and optimise lipoprotein levels.
- Ensuring that disorders (such as hypertension or diabetes) that contribute to CHD risk are managed appropriately.

Smoking cessation

Smoking can substantially increase the risk of premature mortality, particularly in combination with other CHD risk factors such as raised lipid levels.[8] Original data from the Framingham Study showed that smoking has been estimated to increase the relative risk of CHD by a factor of 1.6. Furthermore, the combination of smoking, hypertension and raised serum cholesterol levels has a multiplicative effect, such that the relative risk factor is approximately 16 (Figure 6).[43]

Figure 6.

Quantification and interaction of risk associated with combinations of smoking, hypertension (systolic blood pressure > 195 mmHg) and dyslipidaemia (serum cholesterol > 8.5 mmol/L).[43] Each of these factors significantly increases the risk of coronary heart disease (CHD). When these factors are combined in an individual, their effects become multiplicative, such that the presence of all three risk factors increases the CHD risk 16-fold.

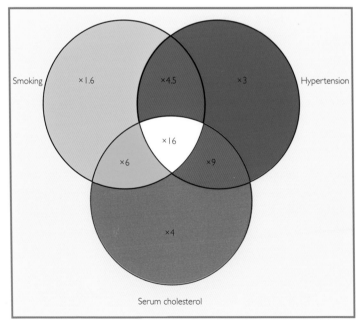

Guidance on how to help patients stop smoking is available from Prodigy (www.cks.library.nhs.uk) and NICE (www.nice.org.uk). A structured programme is recommended, ensuring that adequate support is provided and that nicotine-replacement therapy (bupropion or varenicline) is prescribed if necessary. Support for patients is available from local NHS Stop Smoking Services (which provides group or individual support sessions), the NHS Smoking Helpline (0800 1690169), Quitline 0800 002200 and the website www.gosmokefree.co.uk.

Physical activity

> **Physical activity has many benefits in terms of reducing an individual's cardiovascular risk**

Physical activity has many benefits in terms of reducing an individual's cardiovascular risk, such as reducing blood pressure, increasing levels of HDL-C, reducing blood clotting, aiding weight loss and decreasing stress.

NICE has produced draft guidance on physical activity interventions.[44] The benefits of exercise should be discussed with patients, who should be advised to undertake a minimum of 30 minutes' moderate exercise on 5 days a week. Walking, cycling, gardening, household activities and recreational pursuits can all form part of regular daily physical activity. Exercise referral schemes, pedometers and community-based organised walking or cycling schemes should only be recommended when they form part of a formal research study.[44] Available data on exercise schemes suggest that they are beneficial in the short term (up to 12 weeks) but may not be effective at maintaining physical activity in the long term.[45]

Diet

The current advice from the British Heart Foundation on eating for a healthy heart is summarised in Table 3. These recommendations are based on overwhelming evidence for the benefit of fruit and vegetable consumption in reducing the incidence of heart disease, together with evidence that has led to a more qualitative approach to the intake of dietary fats.[16] Current advice is to moderate fat intake, and to replace saturated fats with the types of fat that confer cardioprotection.[46,47] These include polyunsaturated fats, particularly omega-3, which is found in oily fish, nuts and seeds, and also omega-6, found in sunflower, safflower, corn and soya bean oils (although most people get sufficient omega-6 in their diets). Monounsaturated fats found in olive oil and rapeseed oil are also considered to be beneficial.

Patient education

Patient education is vital for lifestyle modifications to be effective

Patient education is vital for lifestyle modifications to be effective. Leaflets and other educational material are available from various sources. For example, HEART UK provides various helpful fact sheets on cholesterol, healthy eating and exercise (www.heartuk.org.uk). The British Heart Foundation also provides similar information online (www.bhf.org.uk). Advice on healthy eating is available from the Food Standards Agency (www.eatwell.gov.uk).

There are clear links between social class, literacy skills, ill health and poor diet. People with poor language or literacy skills may have difficulty explaining their symptoms to a doctor, reading instructions about their medicines, following information about diets, and may be unable to seek out information that could improve their health. The Skilled for Health initiative (part of the *Choosing Health* white paper) aims to improve literacy, numeracy and language skills using health as the incentive.

Table 3.

Recommendations for eating for a healthy heart, adapted from British Heart Foundation guidelines (www.bhf.org.uk).

Food group	Recommendation	Proposed biochemical effects
Fruit and vegetables	Consume at least five portions a day	Contain antioxidants which combat oxidative stress, fibre which reduces cholesterol absorption, folic acid which reduces homocysteine levels, and potassium which regulates blood pressure
Saturated fats	Limit consumption and replace with polyunsaturated fatty acids and monounsaturated fatty acids	Raises LDL-C
Polyunsaturated fatty acids	Consume in moderation and in preference to saturated fats	Lowers LDL-C
Monounsaturated fatty acids (e.g. olive oil)	Consume in moderation and in preference to saturated fats	Lowers LDL-C
Omega-3 polyunsaturated fatty acids (fish oil)	Consume regularly (i.e. two portions of oily fish per week)	Decreases blood clotting and reduces plasma triglycerides
Trans-fatty acids	Avoid consumption	Raises LDL-C
Salt	Limit consumption	Sodium raises blood pressure
Alcohol	Drink in moderation: 1–2 units per day	Excess may raise blood pressure, damage heart and cause weight gain

LDL-C, low density lipoprotein cholesterol.

Local community schemes that provide education on topics such as healthy eating and exercise could be of benefit for some patients.

Lipid-modifying pharmacotherapy

If lifestyle changes alone do not lower LDL-C levels satisfactorily, then pharmacological intervention is justified

If lifestyle changes alone do not lower LDL-C levels satisfactorily, then pharmacological intervention is justified. A number of treatment options are available, the advantages and disadvantages of which are discussed below:

- statins;
- cholesterol absorption inhibitors;
- fibrates;
- nicotinic acid (niacin);
- omega-3 fish oils;
- anion-exchange resins.

Statins

The statins (hydroxymethylglutaryl coenzyme A [HMG-CoA] reductase inhibitors) are now established as first-line pharmacological treatment for hypercholesterolaemia or mixed hyperlipidaemia in which the major lipid abnormality is raised cholesterol.[48]

Statins are very effective in lowering LDL-C, slightly raise HDL-C and moderately lower triglyceride levels.[48]

Statins available in the UK are atorvastatin, fluvastatin, pravastatin, rosuvastatin and simvastatin.

Statins have proven efficacy in terms of achieving surrogate endpoints (e.g. lowering LDL-C levels). Statin therapy can reduce LDL-C by more than 50% and total cholesterol by 20–30%.[49,50]

Statins can reduce CVD-related morbidity and mortality, in both primary and secondary prevention.[12,51]

Statins reduce all-cause mortality, although evidence for the latter in primary prevention is contradictory.[51–53]

Statins reduce the risk of stroke as well as CHD.

If statin monotherapy does not lower LDL-C sufficiently, ezetimibe can be added to statin therapy.

Statins can be used in conjunction with anion-exchange resins for the treatment of severe hypercholesterolaemia, or with fibrates for patients with severe mixed hyperlipidaemia who are at risk of CHD. Careful safety monitoring is required with the latter scenario because of an increased risk of serious side-effects (myositis and rhabdomyolysis).[39]

Cholesterol absorption inhibitors

Plant sterols and stanols are incorporated into a variety of widely available commercial food products, including spreads, yoghurts and milk drinks. They reduce active absorption of cholesterol from the small intestine by interfering with micellar structure. Eating 1–3 g of plant sterols per day can lower LDL-C by 5–15%,[54] but eating larger quantities does not produce an additional decrease. Plant sterols and stanols appear to be well tolerated. However, products containing these compounds are relatively expensive and therefore are not accessible to all patients.

Ezetimibe is a selective inhibitor of cholesterol absorption that targets the exogenous pathway of cholesterol biosynthesis (see Figure 5, page 9). It acts in a complementary manner to the statins, and provides additional cholesterol-lowering efficacy when combined with statins. Clinical trials have demonstrated that the addition of ezetimibe to a statin can produce additional marked reductions in

LDL-C compared with statin monotherapy,[55] and also produce further reductions in the 10-year cardiovascular risk in patients with diabetes and the metabolic syndrome.[56]

Ezetimibe is licensed as both monotherapy and as combination therapy with a statin in patients with hypercholesterolaemia. NICE recommends ezetimibe in combination with initial statin therapy in patients whose serum total cholesterol or LDL-C concentration is not appropriately controlled after dose titration or where titration is limited by intolerance to the initial statin therapy and consideration is being given to switching to an alternative statin.[33] NICE also recommends the use of ezetimibe as monotherapy because of contraindications or intolerance to statins.[33] The NICE guidance goes on to say that when a decision has been made to treat with ezetimibe coadministered with a statin, that this should be done on the basis of lowest acquisition cost.[33] In the UK, a fixed-dose combination of ezetimibe and simvastatin is available in a single tablet (Inegy®).

Fibrates

Fibrates are particularly effective in reducing triglyceride levels and also have beneficial effects on both HDL-C and LDL-C levels. The fibrates licensed for use in the UK are bezafibrate, ciprofibrate, fenofibrate and gemfibrozil.

Fibrates are generally well tolerated, and are particularly useful for patients with moderate-to-severe hypertriglyceridaemia. However, they have only a moderate effect on LDL-C levels and are not recommended as first-line treatment for isolated hypercholesterolaemia.[39]

Patients with mixed hyperlipidaemia who are at high risk of CHD can be prescribed a statin plus a fibrate. These patients should be monitored carefully because of an increased risk of side-effects (e.g. myositis and rhabdomyolysis).[57]

Nicotinic acid

High doses of nicotinic acid (niacin) (1.5–3.0 g/day) can modify blood lipoprotein levels, including significant effects on HDL-C. However, its use is limited by side-effects, such as flushing and headaches (caused by vasodilation), skin irritation and gastrointestinal symptoms. Small increases in uric acid and blood sugar levels may also occur, and there is an increased risk of myopathy when nicotinic acid is used in conjunction with a statin.[58] For these reasons nicotinic acid is rarely used in the UK.[39]

Extended-release formulations of niacin (e.g. Niaspan®) appear to have some advantages over immediate-release formulations in terms of tolerability, and may enable more patients to persist with treatment. Aspirin tends to offset the flushing, which is prostaglandin mediated.

Omega-3 fish oils

Omega-3 fish oils such as Maxepa® and Omacor® contain eicosapentaenoic acid and docosahexaenoic acid and are licensed in the UK for the treatment of hypertriglyceridaemia.

They may be used in conjunction with a fibrate or statin, although supporting data for these interventions is lacking. However, omega-3 fish oils may be useful for patients with severe hypertriglyceridaemia, particularly in combination with a fibrate, or for mixed hyperlipidaemia in combination with a statin.[39]

Anion-exchange resins

Anion-exchange resins such as colestyramine and colestipol have been available for nearly 40 years and are effective in reducing serum cholesterol levels and CHD/non-fatal MI.[59] Anion-exchange resins are not absorbed and therefore cause gastrointestinal side-effects such as constipation, nausea and flatulence, which can reduce patient compliance.[39] Anion-exchange resins can be considered in the following situations:

- for patients who are intolerant to statin therapy;
- in combination with a fibrate or nicotinic acid to treat mixed hyperlipidaemia;
- in combination with a statin to treat severe hyperlipidaemia;
- for children with familial hypercholesterolaemia.[60]

Strategies to achieve target lipid levels

GPs most commonly choose a target-based strategy for the treatment of lipid disorders. Dietary modifications and exercise should form part of any treatment plan. Although their efficacy varies, statins are highly effective at reducing LDL-C and total cholesterol. The more potent statins and the new combination drug Inegy® achieve greater reductions in cholesterol, and a greater proportion of patients reach target lipid levels at starting doses. Many GPs prefer the ease of this approach over dose titration, which can require many more patient visits.

Whatever strategy is chosen, all clinicians will encounter patients in whom target lipid levels are not being achieved, a scenario that will become more commonplace as guideline targets become more and more stringent. Solutions and strategies to consider for these patients include:

- checking adherence with prescribed therapy;
- checking adherence with dietary and exercise changes;
- titrating the dose of statin (each doubling of dose reduces LDL-C by about 6%);
- switching to a more potent statin;
- adding a plant sterol or stanol product to the diet;
- adding a cholesterol absorption inhibitor (ezetimibe);
- combination therapy (usually ezetimibe, sometimes a fibrate or nicotinic acid);
- referral to a lipid specialist.

NOTES

Practice management issues

Key points

- Responsibility for CVD prevention in the UK lies predominantly with primary care.

- Effective prevention of CVD requires a holistic multidisciplinary approach, which primary care is well placed to meet.

- The challenge is to maximise prevention interventions in a way that is evidence-based, pragmatic and affordable, whilst achieving national targets.

- New structures of care need to be developed with associated quality assurance measures.

- Audit standards represent the minimum standard of care, and the optimal targets should be achieved whenever possible.

The challenge in primary care

Treatment of lipid disorders is now a mainstream activity for primary care

Over the last decade or so the treatment of lipid disorders has become a mainstream activity for all primary care professionals, rather than being the domain of a few interested secondary care specialists. This clearly comes from our growing understanding of the role of lipid abnormalities in causing CVD, the growing burden of CVD to society, and incontrovertible evidence from trials of the benefit of lipid lowering in reducing both morbidity and mortality.

Responsibility for the management of lipid disorders now lies principally within primary care, which, given its holistic and multidisciplinary nature, is well placed to meet this challenge. Moreover, the stimulus of the new General Medical Services (GMS) contract is facilitating the development of the structures of care needed to support the process.

Geographical and socioeconomic variations in CHD affect healthcare burden

The burden of CVD in the UK is large and is likely to increase as the population ages. At current rates, nearly half the population will die from a cardiovascular cause. Different patterns of ethnicity, geography (there is a North–South divide) and socioeconomic status expose different practices to different rates of cardiovascular morbidity and mortality. Table 4 shows the percentages of the Scottish population, an area of high risk in the UK, aged 35–64 years, requiring lipid-lowering treatment for different levels of absolute risk.

Full implementation of primary and secondary prevention strategies will involve an increasing percentage of the adult population, as the thresholds for intervention are lowered and as the age range of individuals to be targeted is expanded.

Table 4.

Population burden: patients from a Scottish population, aged 35–64 years, requiring lipid-lowering treatments for different levels of absolute coronary heart disease (CHD) risk.[62]

	10-year CHD risk (%)	Patients requiring lipid-lowering medication (%)
Secondary prevention	–	8.5
Primary prevention	6	32.9
	15	9.7
	20	5.4
	30	1.5

Managing CHD places a huge workload on primary care

Until recently, guidelines for primary prevention endorsed intervention only at the 30% level of CHD risk over 10 years, even though evidence from trials clearly demonstrates benefit at a 6% 10-year risk. The economic and workload implications for treatment to the lowest level of the evidence base are enormous, and beyond the resources of most societies. Even treating to standards such as the NSF for CHD in England places a huge workload on primary care. For example, in a theoretical practice of 10,000 patients, it has been estimated that 2,221 'disease control measures' will be required to satisfy the NSF requirements for secondary prevention of CHD and primary prevention in patients with a 30% 10-year CVD risk. A 'disease control measure' such as achieving target blood pressure or cholesterol level is likely to require several consultations; the workload implications are therefore enormous.

The latest recommendations identify an even lower drug intervention threshold, at a 20% 10-year CVD risk (equivalent to a 15% 10-year CHD risk), but indications are that the Government will commit financially to the implications of full implementation.[37,38]

Lipid-modifying therapy needs to be continued for several years before any effect on outcomes becomes evident. The challenge of ensuring appropriate follow-up and compliance lies with primary care.

The implementation gap between evidence and practice

Even though preventing CVD is clearly important in terms of public health, a wealth of evidence illustrates that there is a gap between the potential suggested by the evidence base and actual implementation in practice. European Action on Secondary and Primary Prevention by Intervention to Reduce Events (EUROASPIRE II), a survey of CHD secondary prevention undertaken in 15 European countries between 1999 and 2000, showed that the target for total cholesterol concentration below 5.0 mmol/L was not reached in 58% of patients in this high-risk group with a history of CHD.[61]

Many practices in the UK work hard at secondary prevention, but there is still some heterogeneity in achievement despite national initiatives such as the QOF that have been formulated to address these inequalities.[63]

Identifying patients who may benefit

In order to respond to both best practice guidelines and national initiatives, primary care teams have already identified patients with established CHD, stroke or transient cerebral ischaemia and diabetes for intervention. This strategy should also be extended to include patients with peripheral arterial disease, whose absolute risk of a further cardiovascular event is also high. In addition, a huge number of people require primary prevention assessment, which poses a major challenge to primary care. A pragmatic start would therefore be to offer risk assessment to patients with metabolic syndrome, hypertension or a family history of premature vascular disease.

Consideration should be given to establishing registers for patients whose 10-year risk of CVD exceeds 20%

Consideration should be given to establishing registers for patients whose 10-year risk of CVD exceeds 20%. Practices will already have registers of patients with CHD, diabetes mellitus, stroke or transient ischaemic attack, hypertension and heart failure, since these are covered by the QOF standards of the GMS contract.

Adequate assessment of patients is necessary to correctly identify overall cardiovascular risk. Framingham-based risk function charts, such as those produced by the JBS and BHS, are a useful tool; a computerised version of the mathematical function that allows more precise calculation is available on CD-ROM from the British Heart Foundation. A new cardiovascular risk score, QRISK, that provides risk estimations for the UK population based on age, sex and level of social deprivation is being developed. [22]

Developing structured care

The implementation gap that exists between expectation and reality underlines the failure in many practices to develop systematic care pathways for patients who require intervention to prevent CVD. Computerisation of patient records is central to the efforts of most successful practices. Delivery of care can be enhanced by appropriate coding of patient records, construction of databases and the use of templates and call and recall systems.

Protocols and care pathways for the care of high-risk patients in primary care should be established. Obtaining agreement on these procedures from hospital specialists and general practice will ensure that coordinated and appropriate management and follow-up is provided for these patients.

Nurse-led clinics can improve level of care

Nurses have established roles in the management of chronic diseases in primary care. Regular reviews of patients with CHD, cerebrovascular disease, diabetes and hypertension have contributed greatly to the high clinical point scores achieved by practices in the early years of QOF. Greater time commitment, ongoing therapeutic relationships with patients and greater adherence to protocols are all cited as reasons for nurses' success.

Data from the Grampian region in Scotland show significant improvements in the level of interventions and even the death rate at 4.7 years in CHD patients attending nurse-led clinics.[64]

Primary care organisations and many practices now have CHD or CVD leads to coordinate local activities. A number of GPs now work as GPs with a specialist interest, offering lower-cost intermediate care services and streamlining referrals across the primary–secondary care interface.

Lipid levels

Lipid targets must be interpreted correctly

LDL-C is the major lipoprotein involved in formation of atherosclerotic plaques, is a better predictor of CHD than total plasma cholesterol, and is the major target of statins. It is therefore logical for LDL-C to be the major target for intervention.

Unfortunately, however, the majority of practitioners aim to achieve the headline target for total cholesterol, rather than other elements of lipid profile, an approach that is perpetuated by the GMS contract, which only rewards achievements in reducing total cholesterol.

Until direct measurement of LDL-C becomes widely available, LDL-C concentration must be calculated using the Friedewald equation. This requires the additional measurement of fasting HDL-C and triglyceride levels, with attendant inconvenience to both patient and practice.

Records and audit

Minimum dataset

Data recorded for patients on a CVD register should include the following:

- established diagnoses;
- smoking history and dates of advice regarding smoking cessation and smoking cessation milestones;
- blood pressure;
- weight, height, body mass index, waist circumference;
- fasting lipid concentrations;
- fasting glucose concentration;
- HbA_{1C} and microalbuminuria (for patients with diabetes);
- lifestyle and dietary measures;
- drug treatment;
- treatment reviews;
- referrals for specialist advice/treatment.

Similar data could be recorded for asymptomatic patients who are at high risk of CVD, with the addition of a record of total CVD risk, and the exception that treatment may not yet be prescribed. Intervals between assessments are likely to be longer for asymptomatic patients than for patients with established CHD. Read code 44P can be used to record serum cholesterol levels.

Quality assurance and audit

The NSF for CHD indicates that clinical audit of secondary prevention of CVD should be undertaken annually in primary care, and should assess:

- number and proportion of patients aged 35–74 years with:
  - CHD;
  - transient ischaemic attack or ischaemic stroke;
  - peripheral vascular disease (lower priority);

- number and proportion of patients in the above groups with a record of total cholesterol below 5 mmol/L.[35]

The importance and ease of clinical audit of cholesterol measurements has made this an ideal quality indicator within the new contractual frameworks for primary care. Relevant indicators and the points available for target achievement under the GMS contract are shown in Table 5.

Table 5.
Quality standards specific to management of blood lipids for the prevention of cardiovascular disease 2006 from the General Medical Services (GMS) contract.[63]

Indicator	Points	Thresholds
Coronary heart disease (CHD): ongoing management		
CHD 7. Percentage of patients with CHD with a record of total cholesterol (TC) in previous 15 months	7	40–90%
CHD 8. Percentage of patients with CHD with last TC value (measured in previous 15 months) ≤5 mmol/L	17	40–70%
Stroke or transient ischaemic attacks (TIA): ongoing management		
Stroke 7. Percentage of patients with stroke or TIA with a record of TC in previous 15 months	2	40–90%
Stroke 8. Percentage of patients with stroke or TIA with last TC value (measured in previous 15 months) ≤5 mmol/L	5	40–60%
Diabetes mellitus: ongoing management		
DM16. Percentage of patients with diabetes with a record of TC in previous 15 months	3	40–90%
DM17. Percentage of patients with diabetes with last TC value (measured in previous 15 months) ≤5 mmol/L	6	40–70%

JBS 2 has recommended audit standards for lipid targets, specifically:

- total cholesterol <5 mmol/L (in accordance with the GMS target);
- LDL-C <3 mmol/L.

Audit standards represent the minimum standard of care, and optimal targets should be achieved whenever possible

The guideline differentiates between audit standards and optimal treatment targets, which are more difficult to achieve. It notes that the audit standards represent the minimum standard of care, and that the optimal targets should be achieved whenever possible.[37]

JBS 2 also suggests a number of other audit standards for prevention of CVD, some of which are relevant to lipid disorders. For patients with established atherosclerotic disease, these include:

- a record of fasting total cholesterol, HDL-C, triglycerides and LDL-C concentrations within the last year;
- a record of prescriptions and dosages of lipid-lowering drugs;
- patients should be receiving statins.

For asymptomatic patients at high risk of developing CVD (including patients with diabetes), JBS 2 recommends keeping a record of random measurements of total cholesterol and HDL-C (or, where appropriate, fasting total cholesterol, HDL-C, triglycerides and LDL-C) within the last 5 years.[37]

Primary care health professionals need to develop appropriately structured plans of care that will benefit patients and that will also facilitate easy recording of data. Built-in audits that are programmed to update automatically can help to ensure that quality standards are met.

NOTES

NOTES

- The UK has one of the highest rates for death from CHD amongst developed countries and there is enormous scope for more effective intervention to reduce CHD.

- *All* risk factors must be taken into account when assessing a patient's overall risk profile for CVD. Correction of blood lipid abnormalities is one aspect of intervention.

- Raised cholesterol, in particular LDL-C, is a pivotal risk factor in the development of CHD. The NSF for CHD calls for lifestyle modification and pharmacotherapy to reduce LDL-C below 3 mmol/L (or by 30%) in high-risk patients. Indeed, reduction of LDL-C should be the primary target for lifestyle and therapeutic interventions. In addition, low levels of HDL-C and raised levels of triglycerides appear to be independent risk factors for the development of CHD; it is therefore important to assess the entire lipid profile in order to evaluate cardiovascular risk appropriately.

- Interventions that reduce LDL-C have been shown to reduce cardiovascular morbidity and mortality. Although lifestyle modifications are an important component to reduction of cardiovascular risk, pharmacological interventions are usually necessary to reduce LDL-C to target levels. A number of lipid-lowering agents are currently available. Drug regimens containing statins have become first-line therapy on the basis of demonstrable efficacy in achieving surrogate endpoints such as lowering LDL-C levels, reducing mortality and morbidity, and with good tolerability.

- Responsibility for the management of lipid disorders has clearly shifted to primary care in recent years. Key elements of effective patient management include:
  - identification of patients with a high global cardiovascular risk;
  - treatment according to national guidelines;
  - achievement of target LDL-C and cholesterol goals.

- The development and implementation of appropriate systems of care will help ensure that targets are met and long-term compliance is achieved.

British Cardiovascular Society

www.bcs.com

British Heart Foundation

www.bhf.org.uk

Primary Care Cardiovascular Society

www.pccs.org.uk

European Society of Cardiology

www.escardio.org

British Hypertension Society

www.bhsoc.org

Go Smoke Free

www.gosmokefree.co.uk – an NHS site to support smoking cessation

Food Standards Agency

www.eatwell.gov.uk – comprehensive advice on diets for different groups of people

Healthy Living

www.healthyliving.gov.uk – a joint initiative between NHS Health Scotland and the Scottish Executive

Department of Health

www.doh.gov.uk

National Cholesterol Education Program

www.nhlbi.nih.gov/about/ncep/

National Institute for Health and Clinical Excellence (NICE)

www.nice.org.uk

Healthcare Commission

www.healthcarecommission.org.uk

Quality outcomes framework (QOF)

www.ic.nhs.uk/services/qof/

Prodigy

www.prodigy.nhs.uk

References

1   Petersen S, Peto V, Rayner M *et al* (2005) European Cardiovascular disease statistics, British Heart Foundation. www.bhf.org.uk.

2   British Heart Foundation Statistics Website. www.heartstats.org.

3   Mathers CD, Loncar D. Projections of global mortality and burden of disease from 2002 to 2030. PLoS Medicine [online journal] 2006, **3**(11): e442 (http://medicine.plosjournals.org/).

4   Department of Health. Saving Lives: Our Healthier Nation. London: The Stationery Office, 1999.

5   The Scottish Office Department of Health. Towards a Healthier Scotland. Edinburgh: The Stationery Office, 1999.

6   The Welsh Office Health Department. DGM (97) 74. New Strategic Plans: Revision of Targets, Welsh Office circular. Cardiff: The Welsh Office, 1997.

7   Department of Health and Social Services. Health and Wellbeing: Into the Next Millennium. Regional Strategy for Health and Wellbeing 1997–2002. Belfast: DHSS, 1996.

8   Poulter N. Coronary heart disease is a multifactorial disease. *Am J Hypertens* 1999; **12**: 92–95S.

9   National Heart Forum. Coronary Heart Disease. Estimating the Impact of Changes in Risk Factors. London: The Stationery Office, 2002.

10 Brownson RC, Remington PL, Davis JR. Chronic Disease Epidemiology and Control. Baltimore: American Public Health Association, Port City Press, 1993.

11 World Health Organization. World Health Report 2002. Geneva: WHO.

12 The Scandinavian Simvastatin Survival Study Group. Randomised trial of cholesterol lowering in 4444 patients with coronary heart disease: the Scandinavian Simvastatin Survival Study (4S). *Lancet* 1994; **344**: 1383–9.

13 Food for thought: cholesterol lowering in CHD. Oxford: Bandolier, May 1995.

14 Baigent C, Keech A, Kearney PM *et al.* Cholesterol Treatment Trialists' (CTT) Collaborators. Efficacy and safety of cholesterol-lowering treatment: prospective meta-analysis of data from 90,056 participants in 14 randomised trials of statins. *Lancet* 2005; **366**: 1267–78.

15 Lusis AJ. Atherosclerosis. *Nature* 2000; **407**: 233–41.

16 Giugliano D. Dietary antioxidants for cardiovascular prevention. *Nutr Metab Cardiovasc Dis* 2000; **10**: 38–44.

17 Wierzbicki AS. Raising HDL-C: back to the future. *Int J Clin Pract* 2007; **61**: 1069–71.

18 National Cholesterol Education Program. Second report of the expert panel on detection, evaluation, and treatment of high blood cholesterol in adults (adult treatment panel II). *Circulation* 1994; **89**: 1333–445.

19 Beaumont JL, Carlson LA, Cooper GR *et al.* Classification of hyperlipidaemias and hyperlipoproteinaemias. *Bull World Health Organ* 1970; **43**: 891–915.

20 Third report of the National Cholesterol Education Program
    (NCEP) expert panel on detection, evaluation and treatment of
    high blood cholesterol in adults (adult treatment panel III) (2001).
    NIH publications No. 01-3670.

21 Joint Health Surveys Unit. Health Survey for England 2003. The
    Stationery Office. London, 2004.

22 Hippisley-Cox J, Coupland C, Vinogradova Y *et al*. Derivation and
    validation of QRISK, a new cardiovascular disease risk score for
    the United Kingdom: prospective open cohort study. *BMJ* 2007;
    335: 136. Epub Jul 2007. Comment in *BMJ* **335**: 107–8.

23 Royal Pharmaceutical Society of Great Britain. Practice guidance:
    OTC simvastatin 10 mg. *Pharmaceutical Journal* 2004; **273**: 169–70.

24 Quill J. Switching prescription drugs to over the counter.
    Willingness to buy statin over the counter is not related to risk of
    heart disease [letter]. *BMJ* 2005; **330**: 905–6.

25 Haffner SM, Lehto S, Rönnemaa T, Pyörälä K, Laakso M. Mortality
    from coronary heart disease in subjects with type 2 diabetes and
    in nondiabetic subjects with and without prior myocardial
    infarction. *N Engl J Med* 1998; **339**: 229–234.

26 MRC/BHF Heart Protection Study Collaborative Group.
    MRC/BHF Heart Protection Study of cholesterol lowering with
    simvastatin in 20,536 high-risk individuals: a randomised placebo-
    controlled trial. *Lancet* 2002; **360** (9362): 7–22.

27 Yu-Poth S, Zhao G, Etherton T *et al*. Effects of the National
    Cholesterol Education Program's step I and step II dietary
    intervention programs on cardiovascular disease risk factors: a
    meta-analysis. *Am J Clin Nutr* 1999; **69**: 632–46.

28 Jenkins DJ, Kendall CW, Marchie A *et al*. Effects of a dietary
    portfolio of cholesterol-lowering foods vs lovastatin on serum
    lipids and C-reactive protein. *JAMA* 2003: **290**: 502–10.

29 Hjermann I, Holme I, Vrlve Byre K, Leren P. Effect of diet and smoking intervention on the incidence of coronary heart disease. Report from the Oslo Study Group of a randomised trial in healthy men. *Lancet* 1981; **2**: 1303–10.

30 Athyros VG, Papageorgiou AA, Mercouris BR *et al.* Treatment with atorvastatin to the National Cholesterol Educational Program goal versus 'usual' care in secondary coronary heart disease prevention. The GREek Atorvastatin and Coronary-heart-disease Evaluation (GREACE) study. *Curr Med Res Opin.* 2002; **18**(4): 220–8.

31 ALLHAT Officers and Coordinators for the ALLHAT Collaborative Research Group. The Antihypertensive and Lipid-Lowering Treatment to Prevent Heart Attack Trial. Major outcomes in moderately hypercholesterolemic, hypertensive patients randomized to pravastatin vs usual care: The Antihypertensive and Lipid-Lowering Treatment to Prevent Heart Attack Trial (ALLHAT-LLT). *JAMA* 2002; **288**(23): 2998–3007.

32 Cannon CP, Steinberg BA, Murphy SA *et al.* Meta-analysis of cardiovascular outcomes trials comparing intensive versus moderate statin therapy. *J Am Coll Cardiol* 2006; **48**: 438–45.

33 National Institute for Health and Clinical Excellence. NICE technology appraisal guidance 132. Ezetimibe for the treatment of primary (heterozygous - familial and non-familial) hypercholesterolaemia. November 2007. www.nice.org.uk.

34 Pickin DM, McCabe CJ, Ramsay LE *et al.* Cost effectiveness of HMG-CoA reductase inhibitor (statin) treatment related to the risk of coronary heart disease and cost of drug treatment. *Heart* 1999; **83**: 325–32.

35 National Service Framework for coronary heart disease – modern standards and service models (2000). www.doh.gov.uk/publications.

36 Department of Health. Choosing Health: making healthy choices. London: The Stationery Office, 2005.

37 British Cardiac Society, British Hypertension Society, Diabetes UK, HEART UK, Primary Care Cardiovascular Society, Stroke Association. JBS 2: Joint British Societies' guidelines on prevention of cardiovascular disease in clinical practice. *Heart* 2005; **91** (Suppl 5): v1–52.

38 National Institute for Health and Clinical Excellence. Technology appraisal 94. Statins for the prevention of cardiovascular events. January 2006. www.nice.org.uk.

39 National Institute for Clinical Excellence. Clinical guideline: Type 2 diabetes – management of blood pressure and blood lipids. October 2002. www.nice.org.uk.

40 National Institute for Health and Clinical Excellence. Cardiovascular risk assessment: the modification of blood lipids for the primary and secondary prevention of cardiovascular disease. Consultation Draft. June 2007. www.nice.org.uk.

41 Grundy SM, Cleeman JI, Bairey Merz N *et al.* Implications of recent clinical trials for the National Cholesterol Education Program Adult Treatment Panel III Guidelines. *Circulation* 2004; **110**: 227–39.

42 Wei L, Macdonald TM, Watson AD *et al.* Effectiveness of two statin prescribing strategies with respect to adherence and cardiovascular outcomes: observational study. *Pharmacoepidemiol Drug Saf* 2007; **16**: 385–92.

43 Betteridge DJ, Morrell JM. Clinicians' Guide to Lipids and Coronary Heart Disease. 2nd edn. London: Arnold, 2003.

44 National Institute for Health and Clinical Excellence. NICE public health intervention guidance – Four commonly used methods to increase physical activity. March 2006. www.nice.org.uk.

45 National Institute for Health and Clinical Excellence. Physical
    activity – exercise referral review. A rapid review of the
    effectiveness of exercise referral schemes to promote physical
    activity in adults. May 2006. www.nice.org.uk.

46 Kris-Etherton PM, Binkoski AE, Zhao G *et al.* Dietary fat: assessing
    the evidence in support of a moderate-fat diet; the benchmark
    based on lipoprotein metabolism. *Proc Nutr Soc* 2002; **61**: 287–8.

47 Taubes G. The soft science of dietary fat. *Science* 2001; **291**:
    2536–45.

48 Wood D, De Backer G, Faergeman O *et al.* Prevention of coronary
    heart disease in clinical practice. Recommendations of the second
    joint task force of European and other societies on coronary
    prevention. *Eur Heart J* 1998; **19**: 1434–503.

49 Andrews TC, Ballantyne CM, Hsia JA, Kramer JH. Achieving and
    maintaining National Cholesterol Education Program low-density
    lipoprotein cholesterol goals with five statins. *Am J Med* 2001; **111**:
    185–91.

50 Branchi A, Fiorenza AM, Rovellini A *et al.* Lowering effects of four
    different statins on serum triglyceride level. *Eur J Clin Pharmacol*
    1999; **55**: 499–502.

51 Shepherd J, Cobbe SM, Ford I *et al.* Prevention of coronary heart
    disease with pravastatin in men with hypercholesterolemia. West
    of Scotland Coronary Prevention Study Group. *N Engl J Med* 1995;
    333: 1301–7.

52 Hebert PR, Gaziano JM, Chan KS, Hennekens CH. Cholesterol
    lowering with statin drugs, risk of stroke, and total mortality. An
    overview of randomized trials. *JAMA* 1997; **278**: 313–21.

53 Pignone M, Phillips C, Mulrow C. Use of lipid lowering drugs for
    primary prevention of coronary heart disease: meta-analysis of
    randomised trials. *BMJ* 2000; **321**: 983–6.

54 The Advisory Committee on Novel Foodstuffs and Processes. Cholesterol lowering: foods with added plant sterols. Food Standards Agency. February 2002 (revised April 2005). www.food.gov.uk.

55 Mikhailidis DP, Sibbring GC, Ballantyne CM *et al.* Meta-analysis of the cholesterol-lowering effect of ezetimibe added to ongoing statin therapy. *Curr Med Res Opin* 2007; Jul 19; [Epub ahead of print]

56 Sampalis JS, Bissonnette S, Habib R, Boukas S. Reduction in estimated risk for coronary artery disease after use of ezetimibe with a statin. Ann Pharmacother. 2007; Aug 1; [Epub ahead of print]

57 British National Formulary (BNF) 47. London: The British Medical Association and the Royal Pharmaceutical Association of Great Britain, March 2004.

58 The Lipid Research Clinics Coronary Primary Prevention Group. The Lipid Research Clinics Coronary Primary Prevention Trial results. I. Reduction in incidence of coronary heart disease. *JAMA* 1984; **251**: 351–64.

59 Probstfield JL, Rifkind BM. The Lipid Clinics Coronary Primary Prevention Trial: design, results and implications. *Eur J Clin Pharmacol* 1991; **40** Suppl 1: S69-75.

60 Nissen SE, Tuzcu EM, Schoenhagen P *et al.* Effect of intensive compared with moderate lipid-lowering therapy on progression of coronary atherosclerosis: a randomized controlled trial. *JAMA* 2004; **291**: 1071–80.

61 De Backer G, EUROASPIRE II Study Group. Evidence-based goals versus achievement in clinical practice in secondary prevention of coronary heart disease: findings in EUROASPIRE II. *Atheroscler Suppl.* 2002; **4**: 13–16; discussion 16–17.

62 Haq IU, Ramsay LE, Wallis EJ *et al.* Population implications of lipid lowering for prevention of coronary heart disease: data from the 1995 Scottish health survey. *Heart* 2001; **86**: 289–95.

63 Revisions to the GMS contract 2006/7. Delivering investment in general practice. Annex 1: Quality and Outcomes Framework guidance. April 2006. www.nhsemployers.org/gmscontract.

64 Murchie P, Campbell NC, Ritchie LD *et al.* Secondary prevention clinics for coronary heart disease: four year follow up of a randomised controlled trial in primary care. *BMJ* 2003; **326**: 84.

Index

NOTES

NOTES

NOTES

NOTES

NOTES